Jolly Hockey Sticks

by

Doreen Cash Thakoordin

authorHOUSE®

AuthorHouse™ UK Ltd.
500 Avebury Boulevard
Central Milton Keynes, MK9 2BE
www.authorhouse.co.uk
Phone: 08001974150

© 2007 Doreen Cash Thakoordin. All rights reserved.

No part of this book may be reproduced, stored in a retrieval system, or transmitted by any means without the written permission of the author.

First published by AuthorHouse   12/19/2007

ISBN: 978-1-4343-2946-2 (sc)

Printed in the United States of America
Bloomington, Indiana

This book is printed on acid-free paper.

Acknowledgments

This book is for Michael and Jane, and for everyone else mentioned in it.

Special thanks are due to Asim Hashmi, without whose skill and patience it would still be a jumble of papers and old photos in the corner of my study.

DT 01.07

CONTENTS

PART THE FIRST
We'll start at the very beginning — PAGE 1

PART THE NEXT
My Lovely Day — PAGE 11

PART THE NEXT
I'm A Believer — PAGE 17

PART THE NEXT
The Lord God Made Them All — PAGE 29

PART THE NEXT
45 Years Man and Boy — PAGE 35

PART THE NEXT
*Cheerfulness and Industry-
The Best School of All* — PAGE 39

PART THE NEXT
Fame at Last — PAGE 55

PART THE LAST
Odds 'n' Sods — PAGE 61

PART THE FIRST

Let's start at the very beginning

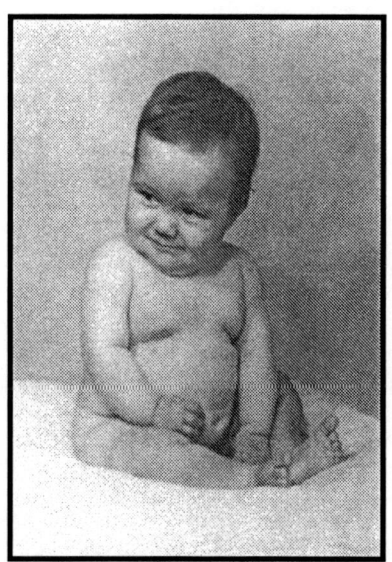

for no other reason than, as Maria von Trapp would have you believe, it's a very good place to start.

Yours truly 1945

Ditto: 1948

By the time you read this, I will probably be famous, this book having been snapped up by Penguin or Virago, or, if you will, some other publishing company. I will have won the Booker Prize, be hailed as the new JK Rowling (DC Thakoordin has a certain ring to it, you will agree) and be sipping cocktails in Max's Bargain Bar in Southend. I will, of course, have been to The Palace to get my damehood for being the outstanding new writer, and Sir Jim will be sitting beside me, basking in reflected glory.

Yeah, right.

I consider that anyone who presumes to think their story will be of any interest to others apart from their close family (who will, of course be drippingly rich if the fantasy comes true - so keep reading, Michael and Jane) must be totally egocentric, or broke. Which I am. Both.

I was born a Londoner and have just done what generations of Londoners have done before me when they've had *a-bleedin '-nuffofit, I went dahn Sahthend.* That is, the posh end of Sathend - Leigh-on-Sea. You will do well to note that I am a retired Deputy Headteacher and RDHs don't slum it. Well, not if they can avoid it; not unless they've had their fingers in the till or on the children and lose their pension rights .

As a matter of fact, Leigh hyphen on hyphen Sea is a place I remember being talked about in my childhood. My Auntie Ethel, who lived next door to us, was forever going on about Auntie Ag who had such a lovely bungalow in Leigh-on-Sea and no-one to leave it to. She and my Uncle Art went down every weekend to clean her house, cook her meals for a week, and generally 'keep an eye' on her. *She's 88, you know*, I can still hear Ethel saying to her sister, My Mum- *I wonder how she keeps going*. In the event, the old lady kept going a good 2 years after Ethel and Art were both dead. There's a lesson to be learned in there somewhere, and if that lesson is to move to Leigh-on-Sea if you want to live to be 90-odd, then I'm all for it.

I'm 2/3rds of the way there already, and the first piece of work that I'm including I wrote as a celebration of becoming what might be called a Senior Citizen, or might be called a number of other things like Crumbly.

My Mum shouts from the bottom of the stairs, "Turn that bleedin' row down. The neighbours don't want an evening with Bob Dylan"

And I say 'It's alright, Ma There's time a-plenty for easy listening.

Me Mum says, at the bottom of the stairs, 'You're not going out in that garb, are you? - Why can't you wear nice colours that go together?

And I say, 'It's all right, Ma, there's lots of time left to shop at M&S

Me Mum says at the door, 'What's happened to your hair? How much they charge you for that? Why can't you have shampoo and set like everyone else?'

And I say - 'It's all right, Ma - I've got a lot of years to look respectable.

Me Mum says in the bedroom, 'That fat, bald little git who keeps sniffing around? What you going to do about him?

And I say, It's all right, Ma I'll be a good wife one day. Me Mum says, 'Well, don't leave it too late, then'

And I say she's got a point; after all, I am nearly sixty.

My Mum in that poem would have to be about 80; in fact I lost my Mum to cervical cancer when I was 21 and she was 61 (the age I am now - spooky). I remember my Mum saying, *I hope he dies before I do, because if I die first he 'll be miserable and make everybody around him miserable.* Oh, and how right you were, mother..how right you were.

I, too have read Jenny Joseph's 'Warning' about wearing purple and I am well-acquainted with the concept of growing old disgracefully - the middle-classes liking to fantasise about the scandal of sitting down in the road when they're tired, or picking flowers from other people's gardens, but that is fantasy. There follows the brutal truth about what disgraceful really means. My father Dad his home help taken away because he tried to kiss her; he was always touching Freda, his friend in her seventies who came from a generation that didn't know how to say f-off to dirty old men; he had his whole living-room, ceiling and all, painted in sunshine yellow gloss and the chappie only took £400. The second last mad thing my father did was to poison his lawn because he was fed up with paying to have it cut but the piece de resistance was having a Hallowe'en Police message designed to deter trick or treaters displayed in his front window for ever afterwards. DO NOT, it extolled, PREY ON THE ELDERLY AND INFIRM WHO MAY BE DISTRESSED BY YOUR KNOCK ON THE DOOR. Daft poster - daft old man, I'm afraid. Part of the problem was that both my parents guarded their past jealously and I grew up an only child of middle-aged parents.

I was told what they wanted me to hear about their young lives - my Dad had been a Hoffman Presser before the war, had married a lady who had not kept proper account of what she owed the milkman, and once you start pulling knives out on one another it's time to split up. I was also told that my Mum's sister Elsie had run off with my mum's first husband leaving the kiddies playing in the street and that my sister Joan, my Mum's daughter, had gone to Canada at 18 after marrying a Canadian sailor. She left in the May as I was born in the July.

It actually took 2 cruel snubs from Joan to make me wonder if, in fact, she was my sister or if she was keeping the sworn secret; but hey - who cares - it is all in the past and Joan is probably dead by now. The worst thing, the absolutely worst thing about my childhood was that my parents, having had to wait until I was 3 to get married, saw me as a vehicle to pay their debt to society; they wanted to turn me into a shining example of the working-class-girl-born-a-bastard-made-good. Apparently, My Dad's sister Dora's daughter in Australia had become a teacher and my own parents decided from an early age that I would pass the 11+ and go to Grammar School and then become a teacher. No pressure there, then. I resented it like crazy and played right into their hands when, no doubt due to a marking error, I did pass the 11+ and I did go to Grammar School.

My father's reaction, although not in the least surprising, was explosive. The whoop of joy could have been heard the other side of the Harrow Road. 'That's that, then" he warbled 'you'll leave us working class behind, now, my girl - you'll be hob-nobbing with them middle classes. Mum, you'd better start knitting, she'll have to have at least 2 new cardigans and we'll go and get the uniform - it says here Juliet Cap is not compul.. compulsory but she'll have it anyway. Then there's the P.E. kit - must get all the right gear for all the sports they'll do' and on and on it went.

For the next few weeks he called me 'the posh gel' and almost every time I passed him, would shout 'Jolly Hockey Sticks!' slapping me hard on the back as he said it.

Years later, as a mature adult, of the bitterest regrets of my life was that my Mum

Me Mum

did not live to see me rise to the top of my profession, although how I did that, Gawd knows. My Dad did, though. It was his debt to society paid off. At my graduation, like all children, I naturally felt totally embarrassed and didn't understand his bathetic simpering - until of course, my own children graduated. O.K., Dad; that round to you.

His parents were Irish and Scottish and, throughout his life, he cherished the dream of going to Ireland, to what he believed was his ancestral home- Cashel in the County Tipperary. He was in his mid-seventies when I was able to make the dream come true and I think that week was among the happiest of his life. We spent most of the week trailing round Catholic Churches in the rain looking at registers of birth, marriage and death to find the essential link - but none could be found. It was only on the last day, when the hire car had clocked up over 500 miles and I had spent all my holiday money on petrol, that he remarked, 'Course, my father may have been a Protestant.'

Eejit.

I wrote this next piece, Sins of the Father, to a Dad who, sadly, only existed in my imagination.

SINS OF THE FATHER

My great-grandfather Cash was a magnificent man, so I've heard tell. A true son of the County Tipperary, he weighed over 20 stones and stood six feet seven in his size 13 farmers' boots. He rose every morning at 3 a.m. and sired fifteen children. He was only ever off work once after his carthorse kicked him in the face. He had to stay in his bed for 4 days, while his elder children took turns to apply cold flannels to the wound, and him roaring all the time about what was to be the fate of the horse when he could get up.

Rumour has it that on the morning of the fifth day, Great-grandfather dragged himself from his sick-bed, drank a quart of porter, staggered out to the stable and kicked the horse up the bum. He always said that the great thing in life was to keep a sense of humour.

Great-grandfather could out-drink, out-work and out-gamble many a man for miles around. To get on the wrong side of him, though difficult, was, nevertheless, a dangerous thing to do. He is supposed to have killed a man in Dublin for beating a little child. Whether he did or not is disputable (though likely).

His greatest pleasure was to sit before a log fire, his great feet soaking in a tub of warm water, and tell stories of long ago and far away. Being an Irishman, his stories were sometimes tall, sometimes sad, but always entertaining. He could make you laugh or cry by the tone of his voice or the expression on his face, I'm told.

Having gambled away his wages one week he was left with threepence to give my great-grandmother for her food money. When he arrived home, she locked him out. Hitching up his horse and cart, he rode to Tipperary Town to buy her the threepenny shawl she had always wanted but been unable to save up for. That week, they lived on eggs from the hen-house, and my great-grandmother cherished that shawl until the day she died.

Me Dad

In their 47 years of marriage, tragedy struck twice. Their eldest daughter married a Protestant and the third youngest son ran away to sea when he was 13.

It was this son who was to become my grandfather.

Little is known of the seven years which elapsed between him running away and turning up at Wellington barracks. Grandfather Cash had obviously changed his mind about the navy and had enlisted, instead, into His Majesty's Army.

He was a dashing young soldier of 20 who had inherited his father's appetite for alcohol, and my grandmother swore he was drunk at their wedding. By 1914, grandfather Cash had fathered 5 children, only two of whom survived the grimy slums of North London. Like tens of thousands of others, he went to the Somme and was among the spared few who returned. 'The luck of the Irish' he called it.

On discharge from the Army, he became the stationmaster at Euston. But not for long. His Irish luck had brought him home only to die. 'A good whiff of gas' the Army surgeon had said, 'nothing too serious'.It was, in the event, serious enough to kill him 4 years after he had inhaled it.

A week after his death in 1920, my grandmother gave birth to her fourth child, a son. 25 years later, to the day, he was to become my father.

My father seems equally unaffected by triumph as he is disaster. At my wedding, for example, he took the groom aside and said, 'You look after her - don't want her back in five years' time with a couple of kids. We've done our bit, now she's all yours, God help you. You'll have to keep an eye on her, though, she's too much like her grandfather and his father before him. Got that wild Irish streak in them, the lot of them.' He was on that occasion, I am proud to say, perfectly correct.

PART THE NEXT

My Lovely Day

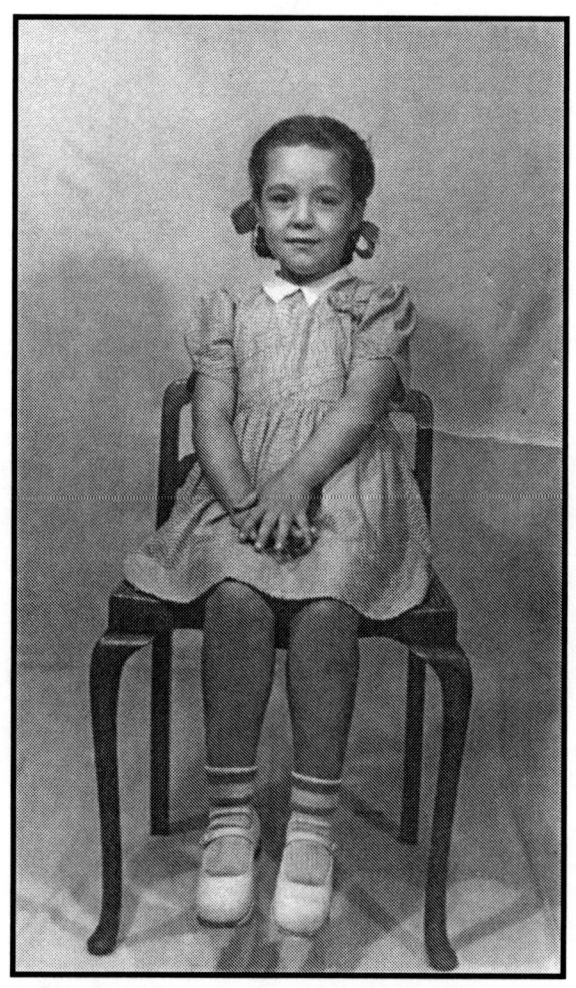

Yours truly 1951

Having spent my sixth form years chasing boys and what should have been the next 3 years at Uni holding together a home and 2 kids on a bus conductor's pay, I finally made it to tertiary education in September, 1970, when I was 25. I applied to teacher training college on Jim's advice and as they were really desperate for teachers, I was accepted. The first disappointment was that I couldn't do French as a main subject and the second that I could only train to be a Secondary school teacher (which is what I wanted all along) unless I did a Science as a main subject. Me, ejected from Science at the end of the third year? (they could do that in those days). I'm not surprised I was chucked -1 vaguely remember writing about people causing disease epidemics by peeing in public drains. I don't know the context now and I didn't know it then. So, it was nursery/infant training and English as my main subject.

I loved English but had not got the patience with little ones to do anything other than terrorise them, totally unintentionally.

It was while at College that I took my first steps into show-biz. It was a disaster. Our group had to do an end-of-module assessment and they chose a bit from The Playboy of the Western World. I was cast as Widow Quinn. At the first run-through I collapsed in hysterics at the sight of the boy who was playing Sean. *Corpsing*, I think they call it. He was a really posh bloke who took everything seriously and looked so bloody stupid in his mac and beret (a sort of early Frank Spencer) that I was unable to speak whenever I was on stage with him. The group got so pissed off with me that they ended the play just before the Widow

Quinn enters -1 could just about manage to rap on the 'door' and say *it's meself* or words to that effect. Then, curtain. Finito. Over. Not a very hopeful start to what was to become quite a career as a superstar of stage and TV Quiz programmes (but more of that later).

One bit I remember about College is that our Group (a different one this time) did some research about which section of the community would be most likely to be helped in an emergency. We pretended our cars had broken down and were going to make lengthy notes on who stopped to help us and why. There was my friend Janet, who was a stunningly attractive blonde, a bloke, an older person and me dressed up in flowing robes like a hippy (which I was, am and ever more shall be). How interesting were our results going to be! We would impress the whole tutor group with our successful research and analyse its findings. We spaced ourselves out at various points along the Hitchin Road from Luton to Lilley Bottom and not one bastard stopped for any of us. So, we had to make it all up. The polite applause that followed our rigged presentation didn't fool either students or tutors - another abysmal failure to add to my growing tally.

It was, therefore, with some measure of trepidation that I awaited my results. In those days, they were so desperate for teachers that any weirdo could pass, so I wasn't worried about that - I just hoped I hadn't buggered up the English Mains. When The Brown Envelope plopped, I was washing up. Hearing the postman, I ambled to the front door, and then saw it. The Envelope. With uncharacteristic calm, I took it into the kitchen, sat down, lit a fag, and opened it. Bloody hell, I was top of the year. Mrs. Thakoordin, it proclaimed, also reached the B.Ed, qualifying standard in English. I had got a distinction! How on earth I managed that I will never know - but I was a qualified teacher who was entitled to go on for a degree in education. On the radio, Anne Ziegler and Webster Booth were singing *This is my lovely day* - and it seemed they were singing it for me!

> *This is my lovely day - this is the day I*
> *will remember the day I'm dying*
> *They can't take this away, this will be*
> *always mine.... etc. etc*

My probation year was spent teaching a nursery class and the Headmistress wrote on my final report - *Mrs. Thakoordin could become a competent teacher with the right support.* Gee, thanks, lady! Actually, I did deserve that mediocre report as I spent most of the year relying on the Learning Assistant, Madeleine. She was a really attractive girl from a good family who was all set to become a Tory politician's wife doing coffee mornings and other fund-raising activities for Our Queen and Country and all that. Madeleine had money, looks and a not-too-physically-exhausting life spread out before her - then her fiance was killed and it all fell apart. She was absolutely magic with the kids and I let her ran the show. What a manager! I knew that I was going to teach secondary pupils the year after so as long as I 'passed' my probationary year, I didn't give the proverbial fig.

I taught some of those 4 year-old boys again years later when they started at the secondary school where I worked . Then they became friends with my daughter at the sixth form college - and what a delight it had been to be able to track them from infancy to adulthood. So, Chris, Alan and Paul- if you happen to be reading this -thanks for putting up with me in your life for all those years. I wonder what you are all doing now, 20 years down the line.

PART THE NEXT

I'm a Believer

Jane

Michael & Sarah

Rohanie

Aoife

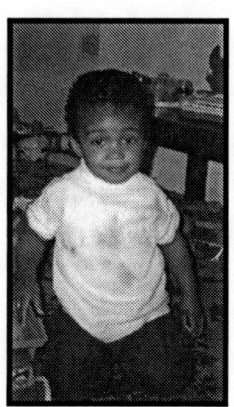

Elijah

'This can't be right', I thought, as wave after wave of agony cascaded over my body like some sort of vile waterfall. Having a baby isn't supposed to be like this. It's supposed to be like the one before. A bloody awful period pain , a naive desire to go to the toilet, a kindly old midwife and a tiny, placid lollopy little angel to shower with kisses and cuddles.

'What's gone wrong here then?' I asked the young, brisk midwife. 'Nothing,' she replied, 'You're having a normal labour and if you don't relax you'll be hours yet.' Thank you. (She had never had a baby). With impeccable timing, The Father sneaked through the door, 'How are you feeling, dear? A bit better?'

'Fuck off

At last it was over and, like you do, all the pain was instantly forgotten. As the quite nice, really, nurse put my infant daughter into my arms, the Monkees were on the radio

> *Then I saw her face, now I'm a believer*
> *Not a trace of doubt in my mind*
> *I'm a believer, I couldn't leave her if I tried*

'You can come in now, and see your daughter'

'A daughter! Oh, lovely!'

He had eyes only for her (he still has, actually) but her gaze was fixed on me. No blinky, gurny little monkey-baby this - her eyes were wide open and I swear she looked me straight in the eye as if to say, 'So, you're my mother, are you? - Watch this space'.

Oh, my darling, I have been watching it ever since and have been amazed at what I have seen over the years. From a feisty toddler to a feisty teenager to a feisty woman to a feisty mother. My darling Jane, you sure are bloody feisty. It reminds me of this thing I read in a book somewhere.

> *My grandmother was a lady; my mother was one of the girls, I am a woman, my daughter is a doctor.*

She's not, actually, but she has a top job with Birmingham Social Services and is the current holder of the 'Black Manager of the Year' trophy. Much bowing and scraping; much fetlock touching; much genuflecting. I have a huge amount to thank her for, I owe her a huge amount -she is the woman I always wanted to be. My own mother's gift of creativity skipped me but transferred to Jane, an award-winning painter and sculptor.

Her brother, my first-born, my angel baby, who is 43 next year, has paid me the greatest compliment of all. In looks, temperament, take on life, he is actually my mirror image. Poor bugger. At least he has a Masters degree to compensate.

When we were all very young

It was because of my children's brains that I was first introduced to the beautiful North Country. As a Londoner, I, of course, think of Watford as The North, but because of my brainbox kids who went to Lancaster and Newcastle Universities, I was able to gape at Cumbria and

Tyne and Wear. What an education! Even at this distance in time, I can still remember looking down onto a Lake District farm as if I had opened a story-book. It was all there, tiny animals, toy tractor and postage-stamp fields. When I visited Michael in Newcastle, the mood was somewhat more non-fairy-tale, non-storybook. Durham University students were all in disgrace because, according to RUMOURSFLYINGAROUND, as a sooper-dooper rag week stunt, they had let all the prisoners out of the jail.

Sadly, I think it's unlikely that that story is true - but I hope this one is.

A man reads an advert in the motors section of the Classified Ads. in his local paper. *BMW, six months old -£5 or near offer*." Obviously a few noughts have been missed out, thinks the man, but for a laugh I'll follow it up." When he gets to the address, there it is, gleaming in the driveway with a notice *FOR SALE - £5 o.n.o.* behind the windscreen. ' O.K. says the man, what's the catch?' 'There is no catch,' says the lady who answers the door. 'My husband ran away with his secretary 6 months ago and asked me to sell his car as they have run out of money.' Nice one, sister!!

However, I digress. I was talking about my brilliant children. Here are 2 poems that I wrote for them - a long, long time ago.

For Michael

Scuffed shoes, tie askew,
Coat floating behind - a meet mantle of majesty,
You come, bearing gifts:
Two sherbert lemons and one liquorice twist

Rain-rinsed, wind-wiped, mud-adorned child!
Were you not so, all the toys in the world would break

For Jane

My little one, enjoy this day, this hour of triumph
When all before you is yours! You have the world today.
You have admiration, praise, laughter, happiness.
Always remember this day.

Don't grow like me,
Who can buy a penny flag
Without the faintest idea of what I'm giving to,
Yet weep over a poor, savaged bird
Call that fair-mindedness.

Don't grow like me,
Who drives on an unlit motorway at night,
Lights a cigarette, travelling too fast.
And, seeing another mother impaled on her steering-wheel,
Cannot vomit,
Call that cool-headedness.

Don't grow like me
Who cheerfully laboured for 3 days to give you yourself
And screamed in agony at a pin-prick.
Call that forbearance

Don't grow like me
Who lives in an uncomprehending vacuum.
Understanding everything.
Call that individuality.

Don't grow like me,
Living in unplanned, unpurposeful chaos
Hoping for something to happen at the centrepoint of the spiral.

Call me your mother.

Grow to reach you daughter's sixth birthday -

Call that love

My lovely Jane was working on my 50th birthday so couldn't come to the Sunday afternoon party.

Later, when everyone had gone home, she rang me from Glasgow.

'Happy birthday, Mum' she trilled, 'Did you get the flowers?'

'Yes, darling, they are lovely'.

'Mum, I'm now going to give you your other birthdaypresent, but I think you'd better sit down'

After that conversation had ended, I wrote this:

GRANDCHILD 1 - July 1995

Bouncing daughter, strapping son
You are on your way into this bad
Mad beautiful world.

You will have for a mother
A woman who wishes you to be christened
In a knitted robe of white, red, yellow, black and green.

Who, one Midsummer Day, ran down the road wearing red wellies
Nothing else. Just red wellies

And who pleaded to have a cock-er-el in a cage.
What's a cock-er-el?

And whose chosen career was that of a sweet-shop lady

And who draws pictures of grotesque women and men
Leaving very little to the imagination

And who asks for cups of warm water in cafes
Because they cleanse the system

And who doesn't shave her legs and underarms

And who drives with the choke out and doesn't take the Pill
Regularly.

Obviously

Should you, quite rightly, think this all a bit bizarre Ask yourself where she learned these life-skills

And wait till you meet your granny!

GRANDCHILD-2 March 1996

Rohanie Therese Alicia Campbell Thakoordin Rohanie
Therese Alicia Campbell Thakoordin Rohanie Rani

Queen of my house Queen of my heart
Rohanie
Ro
Oh, my darling I love you so much!

I know this isn't so much a poem as a roll-call, but it was just so lovely to savour the words of my first grandchild's name, to roll the magic words around on my tongue-bliss!

Eleven years down the line, she is a reflective, graceful, clever and talented child who often appears somewhat reserved, because she doesn't shout her mouth off very often (it has been known, but not very often!)

She will, no doubt, follow her dreams and be what shewants to be - and whatever that is, she will be brilliant at it.

Like most young ladies of her age, she is into pink, fluffy things, fashion and shoes.

For a long time she has been far too grown up for nanny to kiss and cuddle, but Nanny still feels exactly the same about her as she did the first time she held tiny baby Rohanie.

There is no greater pleasure on earth than your first grandchild, and mine's a star.

Love you loads, Rosie.

Rohanie

They say it's never too late to learn; so it was, 4 years after Rohanie's birth I saw a baby born for the first time; in the shape of my grandson, a huge sprog who weighed in at nearly 11 pounds. Don't fall for that crap about God's miracle and the wonderful experience of childbirth - this was gruesome in the extreme. My poor daughter-in-law was knackered for a month afterwards, and has never quite regained her beautiful figure. But as I explained to her at the time - a woman's body takes a long time to recover from childbirth. Take me, for example; my body is still out of shape nearly 40 years after the birth of my last child.

But Elijah - Oh, Nanny's wonderful, beautiful, best boy in the whole world ! Dear, sweet little soul, while Nanny lives and breathes you will want for nothing

> *And so it came to pass as they still went on and talked, that behold, there appeared a chariot of fire, and parted them both asunder and Elijah went up by a whirlwind into heaven.*

He is now a self-confident, self-assured six-year old with an interesting mouthful of teeth and a strong tendency to talk like the Essex boy he is.

'It's well yummy, Nanny,' he said recently as he demolished his Sunday roast with all the trimmings.

Jim and Elijah

His parents are doing their best to encourage him to 'speak properly, but they are on to a loser.

To please Michael and Vi, I go through the motions of being concerned about the Essex accent, but secretly I'm well pleased that he talks exactly like his Nanny did when she was a little girl.

So, by 2000, I had a bouncing granddaughter, Rohanie, and a strapping grandson, Elijah.

Since then, 2 more princesses have been added to the tally.

Aoife

Aoife (say ee-fa), Jane's younger daughter, is getting on for 4 and is a complete replica of her Mummy when she was a little girl - in appearance, backchat, temper and everything else. I know we'll be good mates when Aoife grows up. She is articulate, beautiful and feisty just like her Mum. I love her to the max.

And then there's Baby Princess Sarah, Elijah's sister. Cliff Richard wrote the song for her - she really is a walking, talking living doll. Just gone 2, it is impossible not to pick her up and cuddle her. Like all toddlers, she's a great comedian and brilliant company. Like me, her Dad was about 40 when she was born, so my special mission is to make sure that she has a brilliant childhood, wanting for nothing.

I have a poster in my hallway saying 'Welcome to Nanny's house - children spoiled while you wait'. I've always been one to walk the walk as well as talk the talk.

Both Michael and Jane say there won't be anymore grandchildren for me to dote on, but that doesn't stop me hoping.

PART THE NEXT

The Lord God made them all

Assorted Ducks and Chickens

If you go right down the bottom of the garden, near the rhubarb, you will find not fairies but half a dozen stone slabs. Beneath these slabs lie the remains of the long succession of pets we have had, from Spike the guinea-pig who was done in by next door's cat, to Eunice the hen who survived an attack by a fox and died of old age. There is a place prepared, as they say, for Gherkin, our aged cat; she must be getting on for 16.

Jane had met Paul, her partner, and told her father and me the porky pie that he was allergic to cats, and could we please look after Gherkin and her sister Ocelot 'for a little while until she found them a good home.' And we fell right into it. That was 12 years ago and, although Ocelot went out one night never to return, Gherkin is still with us, contributing the odd 'present' to earn her keep.

Jane once rescued 3 wild ducks and brought them home in the back of her car. Stopping for a coffee, she locked herself out and the ducks in and had to call out the RAC. No doubt the breakdown man is still dining out on the story of the night he was called to Watford Gap services and let this frantic young woman into her car to be reconciled with her ducks.

'There was shit and feathers everywhere' I can hear him saying, as someone tops up his glass again.

The ducks, truly wild, had wanderlust from the start, and were always holding up the traffic as they crossed our busy road having escaped again from the garden. This would have been O.K. if they had remained free and wild as nature intended, but the buggers kept coming back home. In the end, we gave them to a wildlife park near our house –I expect they escaped from that, as well.

We had loads of ducks when the children were little. The first one was Waddler. Hatched in an incubator, he had a fear of water. You had to force him to go into the pond, even when he had his grown-up feathers. Waddler was Michael's favourite, and when he came home from school one day to find Waddler dead in the garden, he cried his eyes out. And he wasn't the only one. After Waddler came Ranjeet (an Indian Runner), Waddler 2 (a cuddly Aylesbury) and Half-pint, a mixture of several breeds who looked like the *wreck of the Hesperus,* as my mum would say. She was a nutcase of a duck who lived on her nerves.

Anyone who thinks chickens are stupid has never kept ducks. They are the pits. They are as thick as several short planks. We put a ramp up from the garden into their sleeping house so that they could go in and out as they pleased: that was the idea, but only once did Ranjeet actually walk up that ramp and that was a complete fluke. Every morning for 6 years they would fall out of their house and trip over the ramp Every evening for 6 years we had to pick them up one by one and put them into their house.

Of course, as every parent will tell you, the kids leave home but the pets don't, and they actually become like sort of surrogate grandchildren. You have the pleasure of mucking them out, the expense of feeding them, and the task of burying them when the time comes: and that's not too easy.

The best ever rabbit in the whole world was called Liberty Thakoordin. He was totally gorgeous, always ready for cuddles and spoiled by all of us, especially Jane, who trained him like a puppy. His 15 minutes of fame came when he was the first rabbit to have bladder stones successfully removed. There was an article about him on the vet's wall. When we moved to the country where he had the run of a half-acre garden, he caught mixamatosis, had to be put to sleep and broke all our hearts.

After Liberty had gone, we felt that the garden was empty without a bit of life in it. On an impulse, we got ourselves 3 hens; well, Jim said they were all hens and he was brought up in the country so he should know, shouldn't he? Except he didn't, and we ended up with 2 sweet hens and one ferocious cockerel. He was called Jack after a huge turkey Jim had once kept as a little boy. " He was a huge, white bastard (Jack, that is) who would be O.K. with me (knew who fed him, didn't he?) but would hide until Jim had gone past and then go for his legs. He ruined several pairs of wellie boots with his claws, and both of us, professional graduates as we were, came to live in fear of the blasted thing.

In the summer, you were scared to make the slightest noise between dusk and dawn in case you started him off, which would then start off every other cockerel this side of Bedfordshire. What a racket!

His end came one winter's night. Getting home at 6 o'clock from school (an unusually early night,

Liberty Rabbit Thakoordin

that) I went into the garden to lock them up for the night. I thought I saw 3 white shapes and closed the door. For some perverse reason, Jack had decided to roost in the walnut tree, and Mr. Fox came a-calling.

The state of the garden in the morning bore evidence of a huge scrap. Say what you like about Jack, he feared nothing. I would be surprised if the fox got away without a thick ear that night but our cockerel was in bits all across the lawn. His head was missing, though; so the fox had at least taken away one thing that we didn't have to clear up.

Townspeople who go on about sweet, dear little foxes being hunted by cruel people on horses don't know what they're talking about. As a matter of fact, I'm against fox-hunting, but not because I don't know what they're capable of. It's hard, though, to hate them when they are so beautiful.

PART THE NEXT

45 years, man and boy

Celebrating our Ruby Wedding

The day that changed my life started as normal. I got up, got on the bus, went to school, stayed there as long as I could bear it, and then bunked off.

Oh, how different my life could have been if I'd either stayed at school or bunked off earlier! If I hadn't caught that particular 187 bus from Wrottesley Road, who knows what I would have become? It really doesn't bear thinking about.

I got on the bus and HE was the conductor. I'd fancied him for quite a while but didn't think he would look at a trampy schoolgirl like me. Imagine, then, my amazement when he asked me to go and see *Ben Hur* with him at South Harrow Odeon. To be honest, and we've talked about this loads of times, to me, he was just another boyfriend who would come and go like the rest. But he was in love, God help him. How could someone as intelligent, witty, charming and totally drop-dead gorgeous as him fall for a scruffy little sod like me? But he did. And, 46 years later, we are still together.

My husband will never leave me; I will never leave him. Believe me, we've both tried.

Like all men, he has done and said some really, really unbelievably outrageous things which have left me stunned. One of thousands of examples…..

I drove into the back of someone one Christmas Eve -just a little shunt. Harking back to 6 months earlier when I had knocked my wing-mirror, he said, 'If you're going to keep smashing up the car, I'll take it back off you'. Stunning.

I saw a postcard in a car once, which said, *It takes a bitch like me to stay with a bastard like him,* and I suppose that just about sums it up. Of course, another take on the situation is that we are truly, madly, deeply in love with one another.

Moving swiftly on, we are both strong-willed people who don't suffer fools gladly and put impossible pressure on each other to meet the standard. Jim is an outspoken, articulate Black man, the type hated by those who imagine they wield power. Unbelievably bright, he went to Oxford and has an MBA among many other letters after his name.

He is a lovely man whose hair went a long time ago, and whose health is not so good now. His biggest fault is that he is too easily hurt and oversensitive to criticism, although he doesn't mind giving it out. On the other hand, the best part about him is that he's wise, resourceful and a totally outside the box adoring granddad. Moreover, on the overwhelming majority of occasions, he is right, dammit!

So next time you're feeling sorry for yourself, spare a thought for this sensitive, clever man who shares his life with a woman who, apart from her immediate family, couldn't give a toss about anything.

PART THE NEXT

Cheerfulness and Industry - the best school of all

A long ago school trip to London. Now they are all successful men and one became a World Boxing Champion.

Truly great writers can introduce people, places and events which make you feel as if you are there, at that time, talking to them. Shakespeare and Chaucer do this brilliantly, as do Roald Dahl, Fay Weldon, Maeve Binchy and a host of others. That's great writers.

I am including the following anecdotes (all true, I'm afraid) about the long ago and far away people and situations which will always stay with me. I don't claim they will be dissimilar from many a teacher's arsenal of tales, but I've put them in because

They will serve me well as research material when I write my next block-buster, Cheerfulness and Industry- The Best School of All, which will be about my teaching career and if I die before it is written, these special people will have had their names in print for present and future generations to wonder about and there is always the possibility, hopelessly remote as it is, that I will make so much money from this book that I will have no need or inclination ever to write again.

Please do feel free to skip the next few pages and go straight on to part the next if that is your pleasure.

June, 1975 - my so-called induction day. In those days they believed all you needed to know was the route from the staffroom to the toilet to your classroom, and threw you in at the deep end to sink or swim. Wandering into the staffroom for the first time, I was met by the sight of a figure sprawled elegantly across 2 chairs with its feet on the radiator. This turned out to be one Michael Wills Toms, who looked me up and down a bit (remember we are talking 30-odd years ago) and uttered those immortal words, 'Welcome to this school, my dear, and I hope you'll be as happy here as I thought I was going to be'. Mike held court in the staffroom every dinner-time and we, his adoring public, sat around in reverent awe while he regaled us with stories about his National Service days in Cyprus. His favourite was the time his mate Tripod David - and yes, we all made the mistake of asking why he was called *Tripod* David, set fire to the field lavatories owing to same sort of paraffin spillage and the fact he had a fag on. Mike, actually, thought of himself as more of a grammar-school teacher than waste his superior talents in this inner-city comprehensive, and after a while decided to re-live the glory days in Cyprus, this time as an employee of the British Council. I remember writing on his leaving card, 'It's Christmas in England, and you're going to Cyprus. Have you gone completely and utterly effing bonkers?'.

Had I known that six months later I would be at his funeral, I would not have chosen those exact words. An impressive start at his new school, recurring headaches and then the brutal truth from his hospital doctor. He was 57 when he died, leaving all his mates wondering whether there ever was any fairness in anything, really. As I say, his first words to me and the millions of subsequent ones he uttered to anyone who would listen, are truly immortal. Oh, and yes, Mike, I was as happy as you thought you were going to be. Thank you.

December, 1975, the first Christmas' experience. How well I recall that! As a newcomer, I didn't feel sufficiently 'in' to go to the staff party in Colin's music room, although I had heard they were legendary. Sitting on my own in the staffroom, I was just about to go home when Colin burst through the door and uttered some more immortal words -'For Christ's sake don't sit there on your own - come round'.

I feel it totally necessary to mention here that the pupils had all gone home. Honest.

Although I was a little reluctant, it would have been churlish to refuse. And so it was, 2 hours later, I was as rat-arsed as the rest, doing the Conga round the corridors with all the others, the Deputy Head included, singing rude words to well-known tunes. How any of us got home without being arrested is still a wonder to me, but it didn't seem to matter so much in those days. And yes, you read right, here is another dear colleague and friend whose words are now immortal. People who were in the pub at the time recall Colin playing Trivial Pursuit with his brother-in-law and a few others. He triumphantly shouted out the answer 'Rossini' and then literally dropped down dead. Being a musician of great creativity, Colin was not always the easiest person to please - in fact he was, at times, 'difficult'. Years after Colin had died, I was in the Head's study receiving a rollicking for something or the other -1 had so many that they all now merge into one. To finish off his monologue the Head remarked, ' Doreen, you remind me, at times, of Colin.' I am sure he didn't mean the creative genius Colin, but the trouble-maker Colin, and it was one of the greatest compliments of my career. Thank you.

September 1984 and we had a new Head, the former one having retired - and still going strong, I'm pleased to say, at 94.

We'll call the new Head Harry because that isn't his name, and, with the benefit of hindsight, the poor sod didn't stand a chance. He came from a very white, middle-class area of Kent and he had obviously said at his interview that he had many, many brilliant and dynamic ideas to take our school forward. And the Governors had fallen for it, and offered him the job.

He looked a bit like John Major - very suited, very grey, and very diplomatic. Here was a new broom who intended to sweep very, very clean. All the staff had invitations to meet him in his study at 10-minute intervals during the first week of term. This itself was a departure from the usual summons to the Head's study. It meant, of course, that he was looking us over - sorry, appraising our capabilities, but it made a good impression on me who the previous Head had referred to as 'My dear' or 'Mrs .. .er.. .Thak... In the six months before he retired, he did actually call me 'Doreen', but by then I had been at the school for 3 years.

So here was I, with an old Scale 2 and not a sniff of promotion in sight. Harry changed all that - not only for me but for other colleagues who had gone unrecognised under the Old Regime. He inspired us; He was actually interested in what we had to say. He gave us back our self-esteem as professionals. And, undeniably he was a ladies' man - charming, urbane and actually very, very sexy. Had Harry not phoned in sick one Monday morning never to be seen in school again, who knows what cosy arrangement could have developed between us? None, probably

I had fixed my appointment at 7:30 a.m., desperate as I was to get in his favour, with possible promotion prospects on the horizon. Uncharacteristically, I slept badly the night before and didn't wake up until 7 a.m., thereafter panicking that I had 15 minutes to get out of the house. I had laid my clothes out the night before - a business suit with just the right amount of split up the skirt, black tights and strappy, but not tarty, shoes. The top had just the hint of cleavage and, by the time I left the house, I looked - and felt- like a self-possessed, self-confident professional. Thank you, God, the traffic was light and I actually arrived 5 minutes early, prepared for The Meeting in which I would impress Harry and make him sure that I deserved instantaneous and massive promotion.

You know sometimes you get the feeling at the back of your mind that there is something you have forgotten? I had that feeling on my journey until I reached in my bag for a fag and realised I had left them at home. That must have been it! No panic, I'll nip to the Brown Owl at Break. Now everything will be fine.

10 minutes later, I was sitting opposite Harry, giving it large about my philosophy, opinions, and the way forward. I thought I was doing so well, using the buzzwords of the time. But I gradually got the feeling that Harry was really not looking at me but at a spot on the wall behind me. 'The man's bored' I thought, 'better wrap it up.' As I put my hand to my mouth to stifle a polite cough, the penny dropped Big Time. Oh, shit, oh, shitty shitty fuck fuck - I hadn't got my teeth in. I flashed him a final gummy grin and made my excuses - to drive back home at record speed to get my teeth, languishing in a beaker of cold water. I would like to say that we talked about it afterwards and had a good laugh - but it was never mentioned again. Harry was too polite, too well bred, too much of a gentlemen, ever to refer to my huge embarrassment again. Like I say, he hadn't got a chance with

the Senior Management team of the time who had been at the school in excess of 100 years between them. But I thought he was lovely. He promoted me 3 times (that's why he was lovely) and his final gesture was to make me a Head of Year, which was serious promotion, serious money, serious status. Thank you.

So, here we are, working with yet another new Head, being a Head of Year. It is November, 1991, and one of my boys, who we'll call Arif, because that is his name, has screwed up big time. He has been over to the girls' school next door and exposed himself 'for a laugh' - his words, not mine. The girl had, naturally, told her big brother who, following true Muslim tradition, had offered to take Arif for a nice long ride in his car. Luckily, I pleaded successfully for him to let the school deal with it, and Mummy was summoned to the school. Mummy spoke no English so my mate Saby, who apparently spoke about 6 different Asian languages, acted as interpreter. From the start I had a funny feeling about this Mummy. She was covered in black with only her eyes showing, which was fine, but there was something about the way she reacted to Arif, calling him *a bastard harami* and bashing him round the head with her umbrella, which was very unusual for a Muslim lady. Anyway, we are sitting there laying the law down about the way to behave towards young women, when I happen to catch sight of Mummy's feet. They are at least size 10 and clad in uniform red PE socks and trainers which probably cost about £100. O, yes, Arif had been little bastard enough to get his mate to stand in for Mummy, but man enough to spare his real Mummy the shame of coming to the school and hearing what he had done. We all collapsed in hysterics after the 'interview' - and Arif never went anywhere near the girls' school again. What a result!

A lot of my work as a Head of Year was working with parents - Daddies, mostly, as our school had 90-odd% Muslim boys. Only once in all my years did I meet an obnoxious Daddy. It was lunchtime, and I was standing in a classroom, looking out over the playground and I saw Daniel being set upon quite viciously by Ian and Mark. Daniel was so shaken up that he missed his GCSE exam that afternoon, but the school still had to pay the £4 exam entry fee. It seemed reasonable to ask Ian and Mark to foot the bill. Ian's Mummy, who later became one of my best friends, coughed up with no complaints but Mark's Daddy refused to pay his £2. 'My son has told me that he didn't do it, and I believe him.'

'But I saw him do it with my own eyes - Mark has admitted it to me and said sorry to Daniel -all we ask is a contribution to cover our costs'.

The obnoxious Daddy said, 'Look, love, if you're short I'll give you £2.'

I was so gobsmacked that I nearly took it.

A couple of years later Mark was on the front page of the local paper having been sent down for 3 years for GBH. I wonder if Daddy tried the same story on with the Police? I doubt it! It gave me not the slightest satisfaction that Mark had got his due. I actually felt very sorry for his parents, who had been living in a fool's paradise.

Most parents do. ' *What is this nonsense about my son doing a roaring trade in stolen dinner tickets?'* I hear myself challenging Michael's Head of Year. *There must be some mistake; another Michael in the class'* I was equally flabbergasted when summoned to discuss him fighting in the Physics class. *"Are you seriously suggesting that Michael has been disruptive in class and started a fight? The teacher must have been mistaken; Michael told me that he was trying to break the fight up. He's such a good boy at home'* and he was, too, the little bugger.

But even the daftest Mummy has to face the music some time. *'O, all right then ' I muttered grudgingly - I'll ground him for a month. Sorry.'*

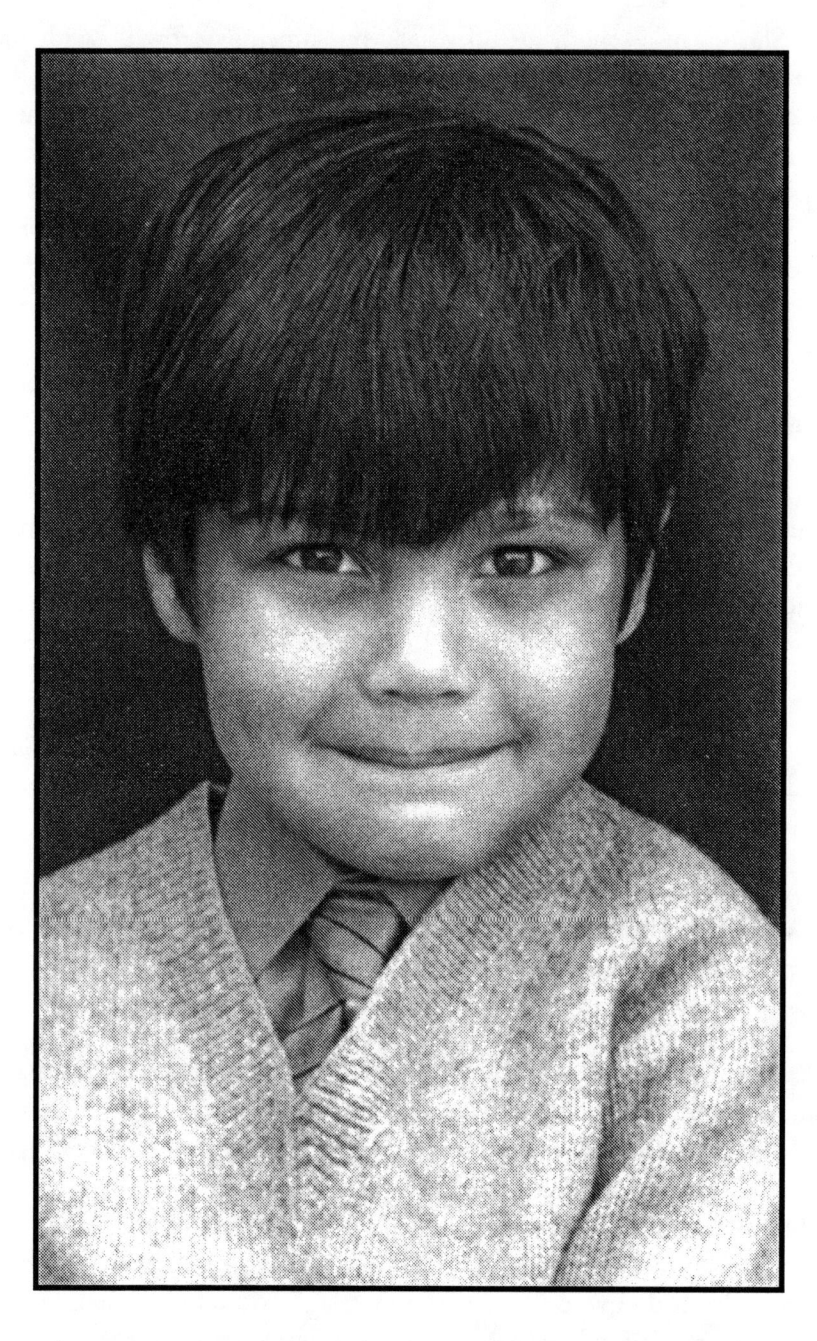

*WANTED IN CONNECTION WITH THE
GREAT DINNER TICKETS SCAM*

Staying in a school for 30 years, you somehow grow up with the people you work with, and so it was that Lorna, Joan and I became the Trio Not To Be Trifled With. We were known, unimaginatively, as the 3 witches (among other things, I'm sure). It was in the days when girlies used to go on diets together, shopping together and throw parties in each other's houses every Saturday night. There would be Lorna in her micro-mini skirt and yellow leather boots, Joan singing 'Cabaret', and me getting quietly rat-arsed. One time, I was on gin and tonic- or so I thought. Halfway through, Joan had run out of tonic and what I was actually on was gin and vodka. One of the many times I went home hammered. I tell you this -1 couldn't do it now.

A red-letter day was the annual Staff *vs* Boys hockey match. At that time, our school were under-16 hockey champions of Bedfordshire, and each Christmas they would play a team of big, strong, macho P.E. teachers. Nobody made any pretence of it being an amusing end-of-term diversion and they all, especially, I have to say, the staff, took it deadly seriously.

In spite of my father's exhortations of years earlier, this was the one and only time that I had ever been picked to play hockey for any group of people who could remotely be called a team .

Circumstances that put us three into the staff team are lost in the mists of time. I am so glad that kids didn't have mobile phones with cameras in those days. I don't know about happy slapping- this would have been dynamite in the taxi-ranks and snooker halls of Luton.

Joan and me on 40-a-day, Lorna with her bad chest, we must have made an absolute spectacle of ourselves. Innocent of the rules of hockey, we were constantly having whistles blown at us, and the boys actually got quite sniffy about it. Especially as the staff team beat them 10-nil. Like all referees, I am sure my friend David was totally impartial, especially as he was Head of R.E. and A Man Of God. Years later, on David's advice, Jim and I made sure that our marriage would be long and happy by kissing the Virgin's balls in Santa Clara Cathedral on a school trip to Spain. Don't ask.

In the days before Equality Legislation, managers could treat people like dirt.

So it was that, after a spell of maternity leave, Joan was redeployed - in other words, got rid of and sent to another school. She actually made a huge success of it and stayed at the other school for a good few years. We kept in touch via Stuart, her husband who was Head of Art at our school. One day, the response to the question 'How's Joan?' was not' Fine, thanks' but 'She's off sick - slipped over at school and broke her ankle'.

For many years, Joan had been living with MS, but, typically, she chose to ignore it. This fall, however, had triggered the disease off and, as it happened, Joan never went to work again. As her condition deteriorated, she shut herself away from the world. Of course, we kept asking Stuart 'How's Joan?' but the reply had gone back to 'Fine, thanks', although it was brutally apparent that she was anything but. At last, Lorna persuaded Joan to see her, and went to visit her in hospital. I was going to go after I'd come back from holiday, but I was too late. She had a massive blood clot which killed her. She was 53. Not fair, is it? I will always be grateful to Joan for teaching me that life really is a Cabaret.

> *Put down the knitting, the book and the broom*
> *Come, hear the music play. Life is a cabaret, old*
> *chum. Come to the cabaret.*

I have, my dear friend, and you are always in the audience with me.

How Lorna could have stood up and delivered the elegy to Joan that she did is beyond me. Like most people at Joan's funeral, I was off with the fairies, but Lorna held it totally together. She is a tough cookie, my Lorna.

When I first started at our school, she was my boss. Very senior, very Glaswegian and very scary.

The first school trip I ever organised was a theatre trip to see 'Macbeth' with a group of Year 11(5th year, in those days) kids. Lorna and I must have taught this very bloody Scottish Play to about 10 thousand kids over the years, and, although I still know it practically off by heart, I get something new out of it every time I read it or watch the video. That's Master Shakespeare for you.

However, I digress. Here I am in the Roundhouse Theatre in London with 20 kids and my mates Wendy and Barbara. The coach had turned up on time, no-one had been sick and the kids were sitting patiently in their seats. I might have known it was too good to last. It was. As the lights went down in the hushed theatre, a woman in a tweed suit strode on stage and said 'Put your hands up if you know the story of Twelfth Night.' I couldn't believe it! From their whole London season, I had picked one of the 2 days out of 25 that they weren't doing Macbeth. My boys still put their hands up, though - when you're in 5B5, one Shakespeare play is very much like another.

Wendy and Barbara were scandalised. What Lorna was going to do to me when we got back was nobody's business. And I believed them - oh, God, how I believed them.

I offered them £10 EACH, which was a lot of money in those days, to phone the school and tell her but they were as scared of her as I was and wouldn't do it even when I raised the offer to £15.

So it was, the next day, I broke the news of my *faux pas* to my boss and waited for the well-deserved tirade. Instead, she said, 'Did the boys enjoy it?' and I had to say they did, because they had (it was a day off school, wasn't it?)

'Did they all behave well?' Yes, they had been a credit to the school and I said so.

'It's all right, then, no problem' she said.

All right? No problem? I couldn't believe my ears.

As relief washed over me like a tropical sea I realized here was a woman so laid back she was almost horizontal, with infinite patience who put the pupils' welfare above anything else. Thank you, God.

I suppose you could carbon-date our friendship from that day 28 years ago.

Since then, we have both had our troubles but we have always been there for each other. And we know that, whatever happens in the future, we will always be all right.

Having grown up quite a lonely child, I didn't make friends easily. I parted company with my childhood friends when we reached the age of 11. Most of them went where I was expected and expecting to go - Pound Lane Secondary Modern School- to learn how to be motor mechanics, carpenters, nurses and housewives.

My main friend at Grammar School was a girl called Kay. We were in the same class in the school sense, but that was all. Both sets of her grandparents had fled Germany with their little children to escape the Nazis - they were German Jews.

My parents were a bit ambivalent in their regard for Kay's mum - their own experience of Jews had been as their bosses in the East End of the 30s. And German..well..that was certainly a no-no! However many times I tried to tell my Mum and Dad that my friend's parents had been brutalised by The Germans (as the Nazis were known to them) I never got it through. However, they tolerated the situation and liked Kay.

Kay it was who introduced me to classical music - and I introduced her to Pop. Kay often went to the theatre with her parents, and I was sometimes invited. On one occasion, we went to the Royal Festival hall to hear The Messiah. My Mum insisted that I buy a hat for the occasion and I settled for a bright red felt. Kay's brother loudly asked me if I'd got any drawers on, and although I didn't grasp the full implication of his question, it sounded cheeky enough to make me 'lose' the hat in the Royal Festival Hall. Anyway, hardly anybody else was wearing a hat.

In spite of our obviously different life experiences, Kay and I remained good friends into adulthood.

Until.

She bought the house she had grown up in from her parents and started an affair with a boy who had been at school with us, who was still single and still lived 3 doors away. In order to disguise the goings-on, she told her husband that both she and I took him to lunch - and to further the deceit, she got her fancy-man to phone me at home as 'proof of the fact that we had all kept in touch. He introduced himself to my husband as one of my oldest, closest friends even though I had hardly known him at school and hadn't seen hide nor hair of him for the best part of 20 years. I was absolutely bloody furious that she had given him my number and tried to use me as her back-up. We have never spoken from that day to this. Sorry, Kay, even though all may be fair in love and war, you can't take the piss.

Daniel, Joan, Lorna, Rory, and Me

My next really good friend was Norah, who looked after the infant Michael while I tried to make ends at least approach each other by working in a factory. 13 years my senior, Norah was more like a mother to me than a friend and her family took us to their bosom. Maybe we were both 'a bit different' - Norah had a huge weight problem and I was the only girl on the estate married to a Black man. But whatever the reason, we hit it off from the start.

One of the many things we had in common was a desire to see Tom Jones live and throw our knickers at him. A harmless fantasy shared by thousands of others in Tom's heyday. I imagine Norah passing on to someone to pass on to Tom a pair of brand new knickers still in their wrapping, while I probably would have stood up, taken my knickers off and lobbed them on to the stage. Many a good giggle we had over that!

As it approaches the first anniversary of her death, I am too choked up to write about the many brilliant times we had. But I wrote this poem for her.

Reflections - 11th October 2005

Those were the days, as they say
Of cheap biscuits and coffee and everything else.
Of long walks with the prams:
Of a beautiful little boy playing happily with his plastic spoons:
Of trying to make ends meet, or at least approach each other:
Of shopping trips to Sainsbury's in Eddie's car: Of Terry Scott dressed
up like Tarzan at the Odeon: Of early, stark and bewildered days
soothed by the balm of your common sense.

All our yesterdays as they say –
Days of simple pleasures-
Like today's yesterday's unforgettable afternoon.

Natural beauty you would have loved-
Warm sunshine (just the day for doing the bedrooms),
Breathtaking Autumn colours in the gentle Bedfordshire countryside
And you riding above, in state, like a queen.

Then, your heart-generous hospitality as always
In *all our yesterdays,* as they say.

Beloved Norah, rest in peace and rise in glory.
We surely will disgrace ourselves in front of Tom
But all 3 of us will have to wait a little while longer

PART THE NEXT

Fame at last!

For the safety of my virtue I shall scream!

After a disastrous start into showbiz as the Widow Quinn in 'The Playboy of the Western World', I thought I'd missed my chance to become a star. But no! Opportunity, rarely knocking twice as it does, knocked 4 more times for me. I was obviously born to tread the boards and sing the odd song to an adoring audience.

When I had my audition to get on the Weakest Link, they asked me if I could sing. Of course I could sing!

'Give me a note..any note..

'Arse.. .arse arse.. .Arse wheat mystery of life at last I've found you...'

I got on the show only to be voted off in the last round because the 2 tarts who remained were both scared to meet me in the final. Bitches. But I'm not bitter.

When my family saw it on T.V., Michael literally cringed in embarrassment and threw a cushion at me, and Jane thought I was drunk, My grandchildren appreciated seeing their Nanny on the telly though. I think.

Strangely enough, I just missed the big prize again the time I was on telly before that. It was on 15:1 and I'd got to the last 3. Then I was in the last 2. Then I had the question, 'What is the English translation of the name of the French wine, Chateau Neuf Du Pape?'

Michael, who was in the audience, whispered to the person next to him, 'She'll know this, she's a French teacher'.

Famous last words. I said ' The ninth castle of father' and knocked myself out. Ah well, it gave everyone who saw me on telly a good laugh. The Muslim lads were quite impressed that I had not known the name of a brand of evil *sharab* and I milked that for all I was worth. Oh, yes.

I was in live performances at school 3 times. The first time was that old school musical favourite 'Oliver!' and I was Mrs. Bedwin, the sweet old servant-woman who finally rescues Oliver from a fate worse than death at the hands of Bill Sykes . The trouble was, I wasn't on until the second act, and spent most of the first act in the Deputy Head's study getting totally rat-arsed with Mr. Sowerberry the undertaker and the artistic director of the show. How we never missed our cues is a miracle-obviously born troopers (or born something else).

Each and every night, as Mrs. Bedwin swept Oliver into her

With Mr. Sowerberry/Potiphar in Joseph/ The Scotsman/Deputy Head/ My friend David

ample bosom, the kid who played Oliver would put his grateful little arms around her and say, *soto voce,* 'Miss, you stink of beer'. Cheeky little sod. I can even remember that his name was Peter and he was a natural Oliver - looked as though butter wouldn't melt in his mouth, he did. Huh!- so much for appearances.

My next appearance was as Dame Doreen in the 'Old Time Music Hall'. Complete with plumed hats, and pearly-queen frocks, my friend Dame Brenda and I would warble all the good old favourites in the finale. Dear Colin, the musical director, told us afterwards, 'You held that stage like a couple of pros'. We assume he meant professional performers.

We did 'Oliver!' again a few years later and I was promoted to Widow Corney, she of 'I shall scream, Mr. Bumble' fame.

No-one who was in any way connected with that show will ever forget turning up to school one Monday morning to hear the news from the Head that Colin had had a massive heart attack and died the night before. It was too late to cancel the show - tickets were on sale and there was little over a fortnight left before opening night. We told the kids that Mr. Smith would have wanted us to put on a good show and that we had to do our best in his memory. The fact that Colin probably would have thought it hilarious if we'd all fallen over was immaterial. The show, they say, has to go on. And it did. And the audiences loved it. And everyone was so grateful when it was all over.

Having considered that I had thrilled audiences enough with my performing skills, I next turned my hand to directing. Colin's replacement, Simon, had produced 'Joseph and his Amazing Technicolour Dreamcoat' at his previous school and thought it would be a cinch to do it again. He had remembered all the pitfalls, the show would be brilliant and he would soar in the Head's favour. Some hopes.

Simon, like Harry the Head, had never been to any school quite like ours before, and it soon became apparent to him that you had to tell the same people the same things over and over and over again before they got it right. To ask the kids who were playing Joseph's brothers why they still didn't know their words after 5 weeks was like asking where the dark goes when you put the light on.

Even though Simon aged about 20 years in 3 months, I loved every minute of directing the show and just knew it would be all right on the night. It was more than all right. It was brilliant. Of course it was, because it was full of brilliant people.

Who knows when my next big break will come? In the winter, I am going to join an Am Dram group in Leigh. They won't know what's hit them. They may or may not offer me the female lead straight away, but I'll be happy to be in the chorus to start with, milling about in the opening and closing scenes with a shawl round my shoulders being a townsperson or suchlike.

In fact, if the unthinkable happens and this book doesn't sell in its millions, there is nothing to stop me from embarking on a theatrical career which is bound to bring me fame and, more important, fortune.

Actually, there is nothing to stop anybody from doing anything they want to do, as long as it doesn't involve hurting innocent people.

To finish on a theatrical theme, Michael and Jane, life's not a dress rehearsal old chums, it's a cabaret.

PART THE LAST

Odds'n'Sods

The story 'The Three Gifts' is, in my opinion, one of the best things that I have ever written. Based loosely on John Christopher's marvellous novel 'Empty World' I can't imagine why it has been rejected time and time again by editors of magazines. See what you think — and if you think they were quite right to reject it, keep your mouth shut.

'Ariadne' and 'Zimmerman from Hibbing' which have also been rejected many times, are particular favourites and the lady in the Co-op speaks for itself- and it really, honestly, truly does make my blood boil.

THE THREE GIFTS

It was getting late on Christmas Eve, and the children's ward at St. Jude's was buzzing. Some children were writing last-minute Christmas cards or adding to the array of those already received. Tracey and Craig were tidying the teddies and Darren, playing farmyards with the Nativity animals. The general topic of conversation centred, naturally, around the possible contents of sacks and stockings, now being strategically positioned as to avoid the remotest possibility of being overlooked by He Who Was Coming. This done, there sprang up, among the older children, an animated discussion as to his very existence. By the time the last of the parents had been persuaded to leave, everyone was excited to fever pitch.

Except for Keith. He knew he wouldn't get any presents, for who was there left to remember him? He could have asked to be pushed to the shops to buy the lot of them expensive presents; money was no problem now, he thought bitterly. But what was the point - no-one would be giving him anything, so why bother? In the seven weeks that he had been here he had, he hoped, made it clear that he wanted to be left alone, was not interested in their childish games. Maybe last December he would have spared a thought for children in hospital at Christmas, but that was then. Before the family trip to London, the Ml, the tanker, Mum's gasp, then nothing for a long, long time.

Peace on Earth? Joy to the world? Child of hope? What a silly kids' fairytale! And he reached up to turn his light off, welcoming the blanket of darkness that would hide him.

Little by little, whispering and giggling gave way to sounds of regular breathing, and soon the darkness of the ward was broken only by the star above the Nativity illuminated by the lights of the Christmas tree.

Attracted to this focal point, Keith's eyelids began to droop, and the star blurred, then grew brighter. As Keith gazed, transfixed, but totally without fear, there evolved from it the recognisable shape of a man.

The form grew closer and now Keith could distinguish features: the sweet, smiling countenance, the gentle, brown eyes.

Stupidly, for he was nearly fourteen, Keith found himself saying, 'Are you Father Christmas?' The man chuckled, a deep, soft sound. 'No, I am not Father Christmas, Keith, but I have got presents for you -the three gifts that you need most.

The first gift I bring you is the strength to grieve: the second is the ability to give: and the third is the gift of understanding. For it is only by grieving and giving that you will come to understanding.

Grief.. .understanding. How often had he heard those words in half-finished sentences muttered by adults who thought he couldn't hear. But he had heard.

Now, he listened.

'You must release the festering cauldron of hatred and bitterness inside you. You must give others the gift of seeing their gifts of love received and rewarded, and you must understand that you will be with your family again, when I decide that the time has come.'

The form blurred again and receded and, as Keith found himself gazing once more at the star, he became aware of a sharp, stinging pain behind his eyes The tears, when they came, were not the bewildered outpourings of an uncomprehending child, but deep, silent sobs to ease his broken heart.

Finally, overcome by exhaustion, Keith fell into a sound and peaceful sleep.

Christmas Day dawned bright and pure. As Keith rose to consciousness, he was aware first of the familiar sounds of the ward, complemented this morning by the squealing of delighted children. Next, a strange shape came into view and, as he struggled to sit up, Keith became aware of the large carrier bag perched on the end of his bed. He leaned forward to reach it and, as he did so, a small ring of expectant faces formed around him. 'Here y'are, mate' said Susan, offering him the bag. 'It's from all of us. A bit of each, like.'

Through tears that sprang anew, Keith looked into the bag and discovered the touching evidence of their children's perspectives; sweets, a toy car, a pink brush and comb set and a book of fairy stories for six-year-olds. Right at the bottom, a gaily wrapped parcel 'from the nursing staff.

'I've got nothing for you - however can I repay you all?' cried Keith. 'I've been such a selfish pig -1 don't deserve all these lovely things.'

'We don't want paying,', said Susan 'But if you want to give us a present, get off that bed and walk to your wheelchair. Go on - try!'

Slowly, cautiously, Keith manoeuvred his leg s off the bed and, falteringly, stood upright. Panic seized him as he wobbled, but helping hands were ready. In agony, Keith forced one foot in front of the other and, after what seemed like hours and miles, sank gratefully into the chair, to loud whistles and cheers.

After breakfast had been cleared away, singing could be heard in the corridor outside the children's ward. Straining his ears, Keith could just recognise the words:

> Yea, Lord, we greet thee
>
> Born this happy morning

As the nurses' procession reached the open ward door, all the children joined in, but none louder than Keith,

> Word of the Father
>
> Now in flesh appearing!
>
> O, come let us adore Him
>
> O, come let us adore Him
>
> O, come let us adore Him
>
> Christ the Lord!

Zimmerman from Hibbing

Rat-faced, wailing little Jew!
Sitting cross-legged on the floor,
You strum the only 4 chords you know
On a guitar which is nearly as broad as you are.
The tuneless squalling that is your 'voice'
Varies in volume only, for you have no pitch, rhythm or range.
You squeak about war and peace, love and hatred
And other assorted social shortcomings

Not poet, pop star ,folk singer or hero,
You are all of these at once
Your songs offend the musical ear, grate into the senses
Yet tear the heart, bringing joy and grief at once

You are an idealist, you say, and will not stop protesting
Until they bury your body.

Fine sentiments, fond, foolish Dylan!

But without your faith and hope, I should be damned and hopeless

Ariadne

Outside the Odeon, in the High Street
Opposite the bus stop, she stands, waiting.
Her best white shoes, with matching handbag
And a brooch pinned to her coat
Make her feel grown-up, although she's only fifteen.

The cold drizzle seeps through to her best muslin dress,
Chilling her.
If she waits inside, though, he may not see her
And think she hasn't come.

She counts to two hundred and looks up the street again.
She'll count to ten slowly, and if he still hasn't come
She'll cross the road to look in the shop windows.

Still she waits –
Ariadne on Naxos

In The Co-Op

It makes me wild- it really does.
I was in the Co-op this afternoon and there was a long queue at the checkout.
At the front was an Asian lady who hadn't got enough money
To pay for what was in her basket, so we had to go through the whole palaver of calling the Supervisor etc.etc.
And that held up the queue for another 5 minutes.
People began to mutter about 'them' and 'illegal' and all sorts of other crap.
And I thought of all the Asian ladies - Mums of boys I used to teach,
Who welcomed me into their homes and gave me dinner on countless occasions.
Come Eid, I couldn't possibly have gone to all the homes my family and I were invited to.
And this miserable lot were worried about waiting for 5 minutes
5 bloody minutes - oh, how awful for them! What an ordeal!
Thinking of all that wonderful hospitality, I, big mouth,
Asked them not to use racist language in front of me –I don't like it.
Oh, Christ, you'd think I was trying to sell them heroin.
As it happens, I'm white - and I don't like racist language.
This business about 'them' as if 'they're all the same'.
How would you, as a white person, like to be thought of as like Hitler - he was white. You wouldn't, would you?
If you really do believe there's good and bad in every nationality,
Don't just say it to pacify the likes of me - bloody well live it!
It's the same with Black boys. People seem to think
They're all into guns and gangs and shagging white girls.
Those that are, and there are many of them, as we all know,
Need their arses kicked. Hard.
But then I think of my Leolyn - he was a Black boy full of life
Who lost it to cancer when he was 14.
And where d'you think your athletics gold medals come from?
What about that lad who's just won the V.C. in the British Army -
Is that brave enough for you, loyal enough for you?
What's more, many - yes, you read it right - many
Of my Black students have gone on to Uni -Some to Oxbridge.

I'll tell you something, now.
I bought a cheap keyring
Of Sol Campbell in his England strip.
To me, that keyring is what it's all about.
Or, what it should be about
What it will, surely, one day be about.
The question is, how much longer have we got to wait?
What makes me madder than anything is
That I wrote this next piece over 20 years ago
In the Dark Ages of Apartheid
It appears that little, really has changed

Hero's Return

I really wish they'd stop that bloody stupid war.
Then, all our young men could stop being soldiers,
Could come home, and live out their lives.
Become husbands and fathers in their own land.
Then there would be an end to flag-draped coffins
Flown home.

Look at this poor boy. Paid the ultimate price at 20 years of age
Only one of thousands of our butchered youth.

Hang on, a minute - what are you doing?
You can't bury him there!
See that notice?
NO BLACKS ALLOWED

Printed in the United States
100417LV00003B/152/A